LATIMER STU

CW01096129

PAUL IN 3D:

PREACHING PAUL AS PASTOR, STORY-TELLER AND SAGE

BY BEN COOPER

The Latimer Trust

© Ben Cooper 2008

ISBN 9780946307623

Published by the Latimer Trust

PO Box 26685

London N14 4XQ

www.latimertrust.org

Contents

1. Introduction

[1] O foolish Galatians! Who has bewitched you? It was before your eyes that Jesus Christ was publicly portrayed as crucified. [2] Let me ask you only this: Did you receive the Spirit by works of the law or by hearing with faith? [3] Are you so foolish? Having begun by the Spirit, are you now being perfected by the flesh?

[4] Did you suffer so many things in vain – if indeed it was in vain? [5] Does he who supplies the Spirit to you and works miracles among you do so by works of the law, or by hearing with faith – [6] just as Abraham 'believed God, and it was counted to him as righteousness'?

[7] Know then that it is those of faith who are the sons of Abraham. [8] And the Scripture, foreseeing that God would justify the Gentiles by faith, preached the gospel beforehand to Abraham, saying, 'In you shall all the nations be blessed.' [9] So then, those who are of faith are blessed along with Abraham, the man of faith.

[10] For all who rely on works of the law are under a curse; for it is written, 'Cursed be everyone who does not abide by all things written in the Book of the Law, and do them.' [11] Now it is evident that no one is justified before God by the law, for 'The righteous shall live by faith.' [12] But the law is not of faith, rather 'The one who does them shall live by them.' [13] Christ redeemed us from the curse of the law by becoming a curse for us – for it is written, 'Cursed is everyone who is hanged on a tree' – [14] so that in Christ Jesus the blessing of Abraham might come to the Gentiles, so that we might receive the promised Spirit through faith.

Galatians 3:1-14 (ESV)

A hard-pressed pastor-teacher sits at his desk one rainy morning, surrounded by books, and staring at the text of Galatians 3:8-14. Let us suppose he is a diligent man, and that there are several months before he is due to preach on this passage. At this moment, however, even that does not seem long enough. At this moment, he is almost tearing his hair out.

Does *anyone* understand Paul's argument in Galatians 3:8-14? It has something to do with the claim that it is 'those of faith' who are the sons of Abraham (back in verse 7), but how is Paul demonstrating that claim? For what purpose? In particular, what does Paul mean in the verse (which must have been the text for uncountable evangelistic addresses) when he says, 'Christ redeemed us from the curse of the law by becoming a curse for us – for it is written, "Cursed is everyone who is hanged on a tree" ' (verse 13)? An avid reader of *Latimer Studies*, this pastor-teacher is concerned to teach and commend the Church of England Reformed tradition. Consequently, he asks whether there a traditional interpretation of this verse that faithful Christian teachers should be wanting to defend. On the other hand, he is deeply conscious that foundational within that tradition is a dependency on Scripture alone. So he wonders whether there might be a 'New Perspective' on this verse (and the argument surrounding it) which is more faithful to Paul's first-century intentions? If both ways are claiming to be faithful to what Paul really said, which way should he go?

How *is* a hard-pressed pastor-teacher in the contemporary church to preach these verses to the people sitting in front of him on a Sunday morning in a way that does indeed *pastor* and *teach* them? That is, how can he preach them in a way which is faithful to how God is working to engage with and change people through the Scriptures?

There are questions of interpretation here which touch on deep issues in theology, philosophy and linguistics – indeed, our very understanding of what Scripture is and does. There is no end to the different headings under which we could discuss them. There is also no end to the volume of material that has been written on these particular verses, and it would be beyond the space we have available even to begin to supply a survey, let alone an assessment. So let us try something different. In this study I want to tackle these verses and the questions surrounding them from the practical question of *how to approach them for preaching*.

1.1. The practicalities of preaching Paul purposefully

Let us begin, then, with this question: How *should* the hard-pressed pastor-teacher approach these verses, and verse 13 in particular, and then preach them? Should he approach it as a God-given poultice to apply gently to the injured souls in his care, bringing healing as their physician? Should he treat that verse as one element within an unfolding story – or perhaps an element within multiple, interwoven stor*ies*, the stories of God's purposes in and through his people – and then engage his people in the re-telling of that story? Should he approach it as one plank in the great edifice of Scriptural teaching on redemption, and so teach the doctrine in the light of this verse?

Put like that, the approach I am going to argue for *should* sound unexceptional. *He should do all three.* He should act as a 'physician' to his people, *and* as a 'story-teller', recounting to them the grand narrative of God's plans and purposes, *and* as a 'sage', ready to answer their questions by expounding from a comprehensive body of understanding. Rather than being rival approaches to the task of applied theology and preaching, these are complementary

3

perspectives on the *one* task of the pastor-teacher. These three perspectives may not exhaust what it means to be a pastor-teacher, but I think we shall see that they go quite a long way when it comes to his role as preacher.

This, then, will be a *multi-perspectival* approach to preaching Paul, with Galatians 3:8-14 as a case study. The main motivation behind this exercise is the great need in any age to encourage preaching which has real biblical substance. We do not have space in this exercise to think about presentational issues – important though they are. But good presentation is pointless without good content and a deep confidence in God's saving power through the Scriptures, which is something we are strangely inclined to forget. As one fine preacher has put it, 'This loss of proper confidence in the Bible confuses the power of the clever gimmick with the substance of the powerful Word'.[1] This is a particular danger when all the heated talk *about* Paul may have weakened our confidence in *preaching* what he says.

The task has therefore been to find a way to approach Paul that may restore our confidence in preaching him faithfully and lovingly by, so far as is possible, by-passing the contemporary debate on the 'New Perspective' which threatens to incapacitate those who get caught up in it.[2] The

---

[1] Simon Manchester, "Preaching with Biblical Confidence," *The Briefing (UK Ed.)*, no. 350 (2007): 24.

[2] While we shall not be engaging *directly* with the debate on the 'New Perspective' on Paul in this study (although some of the discussion will be relevant to it), it may help to give a brief definition, while suggesting some further reading. In short, the New Perspective is a reaction against a reading of Paul in which his emphasis on divine grace is spoken in opposition to those who would earn salvation through works. Against this 'old' perspective, the claim is that Paul knew full well that his opponents in Second Temple Judaism were following a religion of grace, and that his issue with them lay rather in their exclusive attitude to the

pastoral needs are too great to put the preaching of Paul 'on hold' until Pauline scholars come to some agreement (wait for *that* and we could be waiting forever). So far as we can, we shall be shutting the door on all that heat and argument. We shall find it impossible to shut it out entirely – the issues are too important and the noise too great! Nevertheless, the hope is that we can shut it out sufficiently to regain a little clarity of thought.

As we do so, we shall also find the three-pronged, multi-perspectival approach to Paul in this study helpful in untangling some of the apparent difficulties in his argument. If this study thereby contributes in even a small way to preaching on Paul which is more loving, precise, dynamic and passionate, then it will have served some useful purpose.

1.2.   *An outline of the study*

This, then, is where we shall be going.   The three complementary perspectives on the task of the pastor-teacher preparing to preach on Paul we shall look at are: the *pastoral* perspective, the *narrative* perspective and the *systematic*

Gentiles. Paul is therefore not so much concerned with the 'vertical' issue of how one gets right with God, but much more with the 'horizontal', sociological issue of who is to be included in God's people. However, there are multiple variations around this claim, so we should really talk about the New Perspective*s* on Paul and consider them case by case. For a fair-minded critique of Tom Wright's views, for example, see John Piper, *The Future of Justification: A Response to N. T. Wright* (Wheaton, Illinois: Crossway Books, 2007), to be read alongside N. T. Wright, *What Saint Paul Really Said: Was Paul of Tarsus the Real Founder of Christianity?* (Grand Rapids, Michigan: Eerdmanns, 1997). Michael F. Bird, *The Saving Righteousness of God: Studies on Paul, Justification and the New Perspective* (Paternoster Biblical Monographs; Milton Keynes: Paternoster, 2007) is a recent attempt to identify what is helpful in the New Perspective, while not letting go of what is essential in the old.

perspective. These roughly correspond to what is otherwise known as pastoral theology, narrative or biblical theology, and systematic theology respectively. I shall explain a little more in the next section how this three-pronged approach relates to and draws upon an approach to applied theology that has become known as 'perspectivalism'.[3]

We shall be testing our approach on a notoriously difficult and contentious case-study: Paul's argument in Galatians 3:8-14, with a particular focus on verse 13. In this example, the **pastoral perspective** will help us to see that Paul's underlying pastoral concern as he confronts the Galatians in these verses is that they are abandoning faith in the crucified and risen Christ for something else (this will be section 3). The **narrative perspective** will then help us to see what it was they were abandoning Christ *for,* and *why* it was such a dangerous dead-end, leading only to curse. We shall also see that in 3:8-14 Paul himself then tells a story, something like a cautionary tale. It is a tale that is only resolved by faith and the redeeming, substitutionary death of Christ on the cross. (The narrative perspective will constitute the larger part of our analysis, in section 4.) Finally, the **systematic perspective** will help us to integrate what Paul says here with what he says elsewhere, and with what we find elsewhere in the Scriptures, and thereby to help answer the

---

[3] The terms 'perspectivalism' and 'New Perspective' were coined in different areas of discourse and their similarity is unfortunate. I shall try to avoid confusion in what follows by using capitals only for the term 'New Perspective'. What the terms represent is quite different, of course. The New Perspective on Paul (see footnote 2 above) is set up as a perspective on the 'heart' of Paul's theology and, in particular, his understanding of justification, in contrast to traditional ways of reading him; while the perspectives in 'perspectivalism' are *complementary* perspectives on the task of applied theology.

myriad of questions thrown up by what he has said. (That will be section 5.)

Compared to some treatments of these verses, which think of Paul's argument in static, atemporal categories, this will hopefully recover some of Paul's concern to argue with a dynamic concern for the story of God's purposes in redemptive history. Nevertheless, verse 13 means what the Reformers always said it meant: Christ has died to redeem *those of faith* from the curse *of death*. We shall therefore be teaching and commending the Church of England Reformed tradition in our exposition, but hopefully with even greater precision.

2. 'Perspectivalism'

So what is 'perspectivalism'? Moreover, what possible relevance could it be to the pastor-teacher in his preaching preparation?

'Perspectivalism' is the term given to an approach to applied theology originating in the United States, and especially associated with the writings of John Frame and Vern Poythress. The aim of this section is to introduce 'perspectivalism' to readers who are not familiar with it, to show some of its advantages, and to show how the three-pronged approach to Paul I am proposing flows from this way of thinking.

2.1. *John Frame*

John Frame served for many years on the faculty of Westminster Theological Seminary and is currently at the

Reformed Theological Seminary in Orlando, Florida. Frame introduced the concept of perspectivalism in his seminal treatment of epistemology, *The Doctrine of the Knowledge of God*.[4] Frame notices that on page 1 of his *Institutes*, 'Calvin speaks of the interdependence of the knowledge of God and the knowledge of self and then, surprisingly to some of us, states that he does not know which comes first!'[5] Frame considers himself building on and developing this Reformed approach:

> I have argued that the knowledge of God's law [Frame has called this the 'normative' perspective], the world [the 'situational' perspective], and the self [the 'existential' perspective] are interdependent and ultimately identical. ... The three kinds of knowledge, then, are identical but 'perspectivally' related; they represent the same knowledge, viewed from three different 'angles' or 'perspectives'.[6]

Frame notes that 'Within theology there are a great many relationships of that sort'.[7] The 'perspectival approach to knowledge' is therefore fruitful in helping us to understand a wide diversity of theological issues.

Related to this kind of epistemic perspectivalism is *ethical* perspectivalism. Ethics is the application of a *norm* to a *situation* with respect to *certain persons*. Again we have normative, situational and existential perspectives. Non-Christian ethics, says Frame, tend to emphasise one

---

4 John M. Frame, *The Doctrine of the Knowledge of God* (Grand Rapids, Michigan: Baker Books, 1987).
5 Frame, Knowledge of God, 90.
6 Frame, *Knowledge of God*, 89 cf. pp. 73-75.
7 Frame, *Knowledge of God*, 191.

perspective over and against the others. But 'the Christian ethic should present law, situation and ethical subject in organic unity'.[8]

Ethical perspectivalism is actually a sub-category of what we could call 'speech-act' perspectivalism. A given speech (of which a command or law is just one example) is spoken in a situation with respect to certain people (in particular, the speaker and the listener(s)). We can extend this to think of written texts, authors and readers. This helps us to see a vital hermeneutical principle: a given sequence of words spoken in one situation involving one set of people may mean something *quite different* in a different situation and/or with different people. The imperative from a parent, 'Come here!', for example, will mean quite different things to a child depending on whether the situation is such that he or she is expecting punishment or comfort. Shouted from the lips of a market-stall owner to a passing crowd, the same words have some similarity in meaning, but some differences too. We have to take the changes into account to get the meaning straight.

Although our main concern will be with a different kind of perspectivalism, this issue is so all-pervasive that we shall find it re-surfacing at important points in what follows. The words 'The one who does them shall live by them' spoken concerning the commandments of the Mosaic Law to the wilderness generation on the edges of the Promised Land may take on quite a different colour for the post-exile generation of failed-Israel, as we shall see in section 4.4.1. Or, thinking more widely, Galatians itself is an occasional text: a

---

[8] Frame, *Knowledge of God*, 74.

letter written to the Galatian church in the context of a particular crisis. However, by its inclusion in the New Testament canon those words are re-spoken to the wider church to address related issues. Both situation and audience have changed. (We shall return to this in section 3.)

2.2.   *Vern Poythress*

Vern Poythress' deceptively simple book *Symphonic Theology*[9] is an attempt to apply the principles of perspectivalism more widely in theological thinking. He writes this:

> ...we gain insights in the process of trying to see the same material from several perspectives. We use what we have gained from one perspective to reinforce, correct, or improve what we understand through another. I call this procedure *symphonic theology* because it is analogous to the blending of various musical instruments to express the variations of a symphonic theme.[10]

Looking at a specific example, he notes this:

1. Each perspective has a separate focus of interest.
2. Each perspective is, in the end, dependent on the others and intelligible only in the context of the others.
3. Each perspective is, in principle, harmonizable with the others.
4. Any one perspective, when expanded far enough, involves the others and, in fact, encompasses the

---

[9] Vern S. Poythress, *Symphonic Theology: The Validity of Multiple Perspectives in Theology* (Grand Rapids, Michigan: Zondervan, 1987).
[10] Poythress, *Symphonic Theology*, 43.

others. Each can be viewed as an aspect of the others.[11] Perspectives, says Poythress, are like facets of a jewel. The whole jewel can be seen through any one facet, but 'not everything can be seen equally easily through only one facet'.[12]

2.3. Advantages

There are several advantages to thinking perspectivally. It helps us to see when certain ways of understanding things, which might *appear* to be opposed to one another, are in principle harmonizable. They are simply different perspectives, different ways of looking at the same thing. Moreover, once we have seen that, the different perspectives can be mutually informative, increasing our overall understanding. Perspectival thinking is also *humble* thinking; it acknowledges our limitations as thinkers — our finite, creaturely status. Very often we are simply incapable of understanding an issue from one perspective, even if it is possible to do so in principle. We need multiple perspectives to get the full picture. Poythress puts it like this: 'Because of the tendency to human oversight or one-sided emphasis, each perspective is useful in helping us to notice facts and relationships that tend to be further in the background in the other perspectives'.[13]

2.4. Common objections

The most common objection or misunderstanding raised by

---

[11] Poythress, *Symphonic Theology*, 36.
[12] Poythress, *Symphonic Theology*, 37.
[13] Poythress, *Symphonic Theology*, 36.

perspectivalism is that it is a kind of relativism. John Frame admits that, 'This sort of talk sometimes sounds like relativism.' But he then adds, 'Actually, though, it is far from that, and the motive behind it is quite the opposite'.[14] Rather, the motive is to downplay the authority of any one *human* perspective (or 'theology of') against the absolute authority of Scripture. Moreover, it is misleading, says Vern Poythress, 'to say that all perspectives are valid'[15] (as would be true under relativism). A perspective may be false, distorted or simply less important than other perspectives. We have to assess each proposal on its merits. 'The use of a multiplicity of perspectives does not constitute a denial of the absoluteness of truth. Rather, it constitutes recognition of the *richness* of truth, and builds on the fact that human beings are limited' (my emphasis).[16] We should see this more clearly in the examples which follow.

2.5.   Our three-pronged approach to Paul

The three-pronged approach to Paul I shall be advocating in this study is a kind of 'perspectivalism' as defined above. I am suggesting that we can look on the task of preparing for preaching from three perspectives: a pastoral perspective, a narrative perspective and a systematic perspective. We could adopt any one of these three and still produce a meaningful sermon. However, each perspective is useful to reinforce, correct, or improve what we understand through another.

---

[14] Frame, *Knowledge of God*, 194.
[15] Poythress, *Symphonic Theology*, 44.
[16] Poythress, *Symphonic Theology*, 45.

2.5.1. *The pastoral perspective — preaching as 'physician to the soul'.*

Here we are focussed on the *goal* of preaching: the changed heart and life of the listener. This is sometimes called 'application' and, at worst, is omitted altogether from preaching and is often tacked unceremoniously, unconvincingly and unimaginatively on the end. However, we shall find the application and purpose of a text much more integral to its meaning than is often allowed. Good contemporary examples of preaching and teaching from a pastoral perspective include publications from the *Christian Counseling and Education Foundation,* such as David Powlinson's excellent *Seeing with New Eyes.*[17] But it can also be overdone. Simon Manchester comments on one preacher, 'You're on the psychiatrist's couch in no time! — but there is this sad/bad taste left in the mouth that the biblical book was in the service of an idea'.[18]

2.5.2. *The narrative perspective — preaching as 'story-teller'.*

Here we are focussed on preaching the biblical story: proclaiming God's purposes in history and expounding every passage, whether strict narrative or not, within that compass. There are many good examples of preaching along these lines. Much of what goes under the label 'expository preaching', and which pays close attention to 'biblical theology', falls into this category. And we could go so far as to say that the reason why this kind of preaching can be so edifying is that the backbone of Scripture is narrative — that

---

[17] David Powlison, *Seeing with New Eyes: Counseling and the Human Condition Through the Lens of Scripture* (Phillipsburg, N.J.: P&R Pub., 2003).
[18] Manchester, "Preaching with Biblical Confidence," 26.

is its organising principle. It may be appropriate, therefore, to adopt this as a *dominant* perspective on preaching. Nevertheless, this can be taken to an unhelpfully exclusive extreme. For example, a champion of a certain kind of narrative emphasis recently described the book *Pierced for Our Transgressions*[19] (a book addressing a specific issue from a self-consciously systematic perspective) as 'deeply, profoundly, and disturbingly unbiblical'.[20] If only he had read John Frame first: 'Unbalanced attachment to any theological "perspective" can be a source of ungodly pride that can result in contempt for those who do not share this attachment and in division in the church'.[21]

2.5.3. *The systematic perspective — preaching the unity and coherence of the Bible.*

Here we are concerned with preaching the unity and coherency of the Scriptures, especially in response to specific questions raised exegetically or pastorally. Good topical preaching would fit into this category. When this perspective is used alone it is sometimes dismissed as 'framework preaching' and thereby far too distant from the actual text of Scripture to be much use. But a good 'systematic' sermon is far more edifying than a poor or dull expository sermon.

---

[19] Steve Jeffery, et al., *Pierced for Our Transgressions: Rediscovering the Glory of Penal Substitution* (Nottingham: IVP, 2007).
[20] N. T. Wright, "The Cross and the Caricatures: A Response to Robert Jenson, Jeffrey John and a New Volume Entitled 'Pierced for Our Transgressions'" (Fulcrum, 2007), Http://www.fulcrum-anglican.org.uk/news/2007/20070423wright.cfm?doc=205.
[21] Frame, *Knowledge of God*, 211.

2.5.4. *An illustration.*

We shall see these perspectives in action with respect to Galatians 3:8-14 in the rest of the study, but to illustrate how they might work together rather than as rivals, consider the following scenario. The coach at a junior soccer club wishes to teach his players about certain skills, and to keep their wandering attention he does so by means of true stories about a famous past member of the club called Bob. On one occasion he tells of how, in the practice session for Stepney United, striker Bob was distraught after weaving his way expertly around two defenders, but having his shot at goal blocked by a third. A little later, the coach tells a follow-up story. Facing a similar situation in a real match the next day, Bob weaved his way through the defenders, anticipated much better, and scored.

If the coach is an effective speaker, then his young players will sub-consciously be using all three of our perspectives. They will be integrating those two stories into an over-arching story about Bob growing in his anticipation and scoring ability. They will be thinking through how the second story builds upon or depends upon the first. They are engaging in what we might call 'narrative Bobology'. They will also be building a composite picture of various elements in the story, especially concerning Bob himself. They will be concluding 'Bob is a striker'. When they ask themselves, 'Does Bob always score?' the answer is: 'No — not always.' They are engaging in 'systematic Bobology'. As they listen, they will be identifying with the psychological and practical issues surrounding low scoring rates. They will be learning better anticipation, using Bob's example as a starting point. They are engaging in (or benefiting from) 'pastoral Bobology'.

It should be clear that these exercises are related. If

you are unable to answer questions about Bob, then you have not understood the story. If you have learned nothing about anticipation, then you have not understood the *point* of the story (and therefore have not actually understood the story). To put it the other way around: to answer questions, or make 'integrated statements' about Bob, or to learn about anticipation from those stories, very often you need to think about the flow of those stories — or you will almost inevitably make mistakes. I say 'very often' because there will be some questions where the answers are just obvious without having to think about the story much at all. For the question 'For whom does Bob play?' we can answer 'Stepney United' pretty directly without having to go laboriously through the whole story from start to finish. But generally speaking, we shall want to check that our answers are consistent with the flow of the story and do not take things out of context.

It is similar when we turn to the Bible. The backbone of the Bible is narrative — it is the story of redemption accomplished by God in Jesus Christ. However, God clearly expects us to be able to answer questions about him and his dealings with the world from that story. Indeed, the biblical authors often model that for us — making general statements about God within the context of the bigger story.[22] What is more, the Bible is given to us for a purpose. God speaks, his Spirit works, his people draw closer in praise. Miss the *point* of the story and we have, well, missed the point!

---

[22] Moreover, we are often expected to do that ourselves. Jesus, for example, in Mark chapter 12 seems to expect us to be able to give the question, 'Is there a general resurrection from the dead?' an emphatic 'Yes!' How so? Through an intelligent reading of certain verses within the biblical narrative about Abraham, Isaac and Jacob.

Systematic theology, pastoral theology and narrative theology should be complementary exercises. They are three perspectives on the one task.

2.6. Putting 'perspectivalism' into practice

In one sense, there is nothing new in this section. Classical Puritan preaching, for example, always sought a balance between exposition, doctrine and application (although there were dangers in seeing those sequentially rather than working in parallel). Most thoughtful theologians would consider the different theological disciplines to be complementary rather than in conflict. Take Peter Jensen, for instance: 'Unless biblical [or narrative] theology is the fundamental source and norm of doctrine, it will lose touch with the truth; likewise, biblical theology depends for its very existence on doctrine, and is not able to stand alone'.[23] Much of what has been said here parallels the fuller discussion by John Frame.[24] It should sound obvious.

So the principles of perspectivalism are 'out there', but are they being put into practice in the preaching of Paul? I would like to suggest that in general they are not, and that our preaching of Paul would benefit hugely if they were. Some Reformed treatments of Paul, especially in popular exposition, have lacked the narrative perspective, occasionally thinking too much in rigid atemporal categories. On the other hand, the more recent 'New Perspective' treatments, while more sensitive to the narrative perspective, have tended

---

[23] Peter Jensen, "Teaching Doctrine as Part of the Pastor's Role," in *Interpreting God's Plan: Biblical Theology and the Pastor* (ed. R. J. Gibson; Adelaide: Openbook and Paternoster Press, 1998), 74.
[24] Frame, *Knowledge of God*, 206–12.

to be woefully unreflective in questioning both their internal consistency and their relation to the wider canon of Scripture. The result has been a great diversity of answers to some key exegetical and pastoral questions, some of which have been fairly wild. And both approaches have tended to leave the pastoral perspective to one side (and thereby God's people underfed).

The hope is that multi-perspectival approach might bring some balance to all this. And that is what we are to test in what follows, beginning with the pastoral perspective.

3.   Preaching Paul as Pastor

We turn now to testing out our three-pronged approach to Paul on 3:8-14, beginning with the pastoral perspective. Why are we beginning here, with the pastoral perspective? It seems at first a dangerous place to begin. Are we not in danger of 'fixing' our pastoral aims too early, and twisting our interpretation to suit? After all, most of the hard work with the actual text of Galatians will happen in the next section, as we consider the narrative flow of Paul's argument in Galatians 3:8-14. But so long as we do not 'fix' our pastoral aims at the point, this is a sensible place to orientate ourselves and get ready. Pastoral purpose and interpretation depend on one another to a degree that is often neglected and it is wise to be self-aware about that. Moreover, I suggested in the last section that in many treatments of Paul the pastoral perspective is put to one side. While this is a serious neglect in written treatments of Paul, it will show itself most keenly in the *preaching* of Paul. When a preacher stands to speak, he is automatically in a pastoral situation, engaged in a pastoral activity. Whatever he does, he will be making a pastoral statement of some kind, even if he is (through neglecting to think about it) implying he does not care. But if he wants to preach Paul faithfully, we would expect his pastoral concern to be strong and to line up somehow with Paul's.

Take the great preacher Charles Spurgeon, preaching in the latter half of the nineteenth century a sermon on Galatians under the title *The Curse Removed*.[25] His text was Galatians 3:13: 'Christ hath redeemed us from the curse of the law, etc. ' The sermon had three main points (of course). First, *the curse of the law*. 'All who sin against the law are cursed,' boomed Spurgeon; 'all who rebel against its commands are cursed — cursed instantly, cursed terribly.' He explained at some length that he was taking the curse as universal, as just, as fearful, and as a present reality. Secondly, *the curse removed*. 'Some of you, my dear friends,' he said in an aside, 'will be able to follow me in your experience, while I remind you how it was, that in your salvation Christ removed the curse.' Thirdly, *the great substitute who removed it:* '...vengeance is satisfied, because Christ has paid the full penalty of all his people's guilt.' Then Spurgeon turned to his listeners with a final main question: 'How many among us can say, that "Christ hath redeemed us from the curse of the law, having been made a curse for us?".' Spurgeon then fired question after question at those who could not say this, finishing with an answer to the question, 'What must I do to be saved?'

There is no doubt that this is someone deeply involved

---

[25] Charles H. Spurgeon, "The Curse Removed," *Metropolitan Tabernacle Pulpit* 57 (1911). (Sermon No. 3254.) The only is indication of its date of original delivery is a note saying 'Delivered by C. H. Spurgeon more than half a century ago.'

in a pastoral activity, and no doubting Spurgeon's pastoral passion and, indeed, *com*passion for his listeners. There is also no doubting where his pastoral focus is. Despite at least one aside to fellow Christians, it is very firmly on the *unredeemed.* And there is no doubt either how much his interpretation of the text lines up (or is made to line up?) with that focus.

So Spurgeon's pastoral concern was strong. However, the question is: how well did it line up with *Paul's* pastoral concern? I think we shall see that the answer to that is: 'Not very well' (although there is some connection). What is more, I am going to suggest below that thinking through Paul's pastoral perspective more clearly will help us unlock the main thrust of the letter. I am going to argue that Paul's *main* pastoral concern is his fear that people he loves are abandoning Christ (through whom alone comes life with God — and everything associated with that) for *something else,* and are thereby placing themselves in great danger. Not only will that set an appropriate backdrop for the more detailed analysis of 3:8-14 to come, it will help us here to begin to think through the pastoral purpose of preaching this letter to non-Galatians today.

So while we are not expecting to be able to say everything at this point, and we shall certainly come back to the pastoral perspective later, in the conclusion, Galatians *is* a pastoral letter, and it makes sense to begin with that. Before we proceed, let me lay down two guidelines to direct the discussion.

3.1. Guideline 1: Let us not separate 'meaning' from 'application'

It has become a dangerous habit amongst some interpreters

(and perhaps most popular interpretation) to separate 'meaning' from 'application'. But this will not do. Text is written for a purpose — especially biblical text. If I say to you, 'Get up and get out: the building is on fire,' and all you do is correctly identify the syntactical relations between those words and their grammatical usage in light of the various lexical options, *but that is all*, then I am very likely to have to repeat myself because you clearly have not understood me. At the very least this string of words should prompt some thoughts in you, such as, 'Who are you?', 'Are you trustworthy?', 'Is this for real?', 'Which way is out?' and so forth. If I do not receive *some* response (i.e. there is no 'application'), even if it is, 'What are you talking about? — we're in the middle of a field,' then I cannot rightly conclude you have grasped my meaning.

John Frame puts in like this:

> Every request for 'meaning' is a request for an application because whenever we ask for the 'meaning' of a passage we are expressing a lack in ourselves, an ignorance, an inability to use the passage. ... Similarly, every request for an 'application' is a request for meaning; the one who asks doesn't understand the passage to use it himself. ... There is, in fact, no important distinction to be made at all between *meaning* and *application,* and so I shall use them interchangeably.[26]

Writing on the same subject (but couched in terms of the relation between meaning and *significance*), Kevin Vanhoozer would not go this far: 'with regard to interpretation,' he says, 'the meaning/significance distinction

---

[26] Frame, *Knowledge of God*, 83.

continues to be both meaningful and highly significant'.[27] Nevertheless, the two are inseparable and strongly related. Meaning relates to a 'completed action', an 'author's intended communicative act'; while significance relates to the 'ongoing intentional or unintentional consequences' of that act'.[28]

Either way, we may say that by beginning with the pastoral perspective, we are beginning the task of understanding; and if we ever discard the pastoral perspective, then we have left the task of understanding behind.

3.2. Guideline 2: Let us not forget the nature of the Galatian 'communication event', then and now

So we want to be thinking about 'application' and contemporary relevance from the word 'Go'. However, Galatians is an occasional text, a letter, what is sometimes called a 'communication event', between Paul and the Galatians — with what appear to be well-defined boundaries.

What we need to do, therefore, is think through the sense that Galatians is a text written *for* the Christian community today. It goes like this, I think: The author of a letter may choose to publish publicly what was originally private correspondence. This generates a *new* communication event, but one very tightly connected to the original communication event. It has the form, 'As I was saying to *x*, so I say to *y*.' (We have still to discern the boundaries of *y*, of course.)

---

[27]Kevin J. Vanhoozer, Is *There a Meaning in This Text? The Bible, the Reader and the Morality of Literary Knowledge* (Leicester: IVP/Apollos, 1998), 260.
[28] Vanhoozer, Is *There a Meaning in This Text?* 262.

It does not much matter whether we think of Paul himself making his letter to the Galatians public, or 'the church' (in the apostolic age, with implicit apostolic authority) re-issuing it on his behalf. And if the re-issuing has the (implicit) command, 'And pass this on to the next generation,' we have a *succession* of communication events, all tightly linked to the original.

As Francis Watson puts it, 'the Bible embraces writings in a variety of literary genres, but these genres are transformed by the fact of canonization. ... Genre is determined not only by a text's intrinsic characteristics but also by its communal usage'.[29] However we understand the process of canonization, part of its function has been to generate new communication events within the Christian community.

3.3. *Paul's pastoral focus, his anguish, and an important key to the letter*

With those guidelines in mind, let us turn to Paul's pastoral focus in this letter. In contrast to Spurgeon, Paul's pastoral focus is quite clearly on *the redeemed.* Moreover, his pastoral anguish for them is one of the dominant characteristics of the letter. Take the following selection of quotations:

> (1:6) I am astonished that you are so quickly deserting him who called you in the grace of Christ and are turning to a different gospel —

> (3:3) Are you so foolish? Having begun by the Spirit, are you now being perfected by the flesh?

---

[29] Francis Watson, Text, Church and World: Biblical Interpretation in Theological Perspective (Grand Rapids, Michigan: Eerdmans, 1994), 4.

(4:9) But now that you have come to know God, or rather to be known by God, how can you turn back to the weak and worthless elementary principles of the world, whose slaves you want to be once more?

(4:19) ...my little children, for whom I am again in the anguish of childbirth until Christ is formed in you!

(5:4) You are severed from Christ, you who would be justified by the law; you have fallen away from grace.

(6:12, 14) It is those who want to make a good showing in the flesh who would force you to be circumcised, and only in order that they may not be persecuted for the cross of Christ. [...] But far be it from me to boast except in the cross of our Lord Jesus Christ...

What is the problem? They are deserting God, turning from the gospel of Jesus preached by Paul (1:6, 11-12), turning from what was worked in them by the Spirit (3:2), turning back to 'the weak and worthless elementary principles of the world' (4:9).[30] They are in a state now such that Christ needs to be

---

[30] This phrase is debated, but would seem to refer at least to what the Galatians trusted before they came to Christ: the objects of their 'pre-Christian religious experiences' (Richard N. Longenecker, *Galatians* [Word Biblical Commentary Vol. 41; Dallas, Texas: Word Books, 1990], 181). Martyn goes further, concluding that Paul is talking about the Galatians returning to a veneration of the 'elements of the cosmos,' consisting of 'elemental pairs of opposites', the most important being the 'opposites' of Jew and Gentile (J. Louis Martyn, *Galatians: A New Translation and Commentary* [The Anchor Bible Vol. 33A; New York: Doubleday, 1997], 404). Betz, summarising 'a large number of scholarly investigations', suggests something darker: 'demonic forces which constitute and control "this evil aeon" (1:4)' (Hans Dieter Betz, *Galatians: A Commentary on Paul's Letter to the Churches in Galatia* [Hermeneia; Philadelphia: Fortress Press, 1979], 204). But perhaps it is safer not to be so specific. That is, 'elementary principles of the world' covers 'all the things in which man places his trust apart from the living God revealed in Christ; they become his gods, and he becomes their slave' (Hans-Helmut Esser, *Law*, vol. 2 of *New International Dictionary of New Testament Theology*, 453).

formed in them afresh (4:19). And they are being severed from Christ and the sovereign grace of God by those ashamed of the cross, fearful of persecution because of it, 'boasting' in something else (5:4; 6:12, 14; cf. 5:11-12). Paul's main pastoral concern is therefore his fear that people he loves are *abandoning Christ* (for something else) and are thereby placing themselves in great danger.

Those doing the severing are described by Paul as those 'of the works of the law' (3:10). There is of course a huge debate about the phrase 'works of the law'. The phrase itself does little more than suggest *some* sort of association with activity prescribed in the Mosaic Law, without saying precisely *what* sort — apart from the fact that we also know that these people were insisting upon circumcision. I shall say some more later as to what I think (this comes more from the way the argument works than anything else). But it may actually be useful for us non-Galatians that Paul has left the phrase slightly vague if the key concern is abandoning Christ, of which being 'of works of law' is only one of many possible expressions.

The major pastoral problem which overshadows all other pastoral problems is therefore either not having Christ or abandoning Christ. To put it another way, Sanders was right when he said that for Paul, 'God's salvation in Christ alone provides salvation and makes everything else seem, in fact actually *be* worthless'.[31] This applies to what Paul's opponents in Galatia were teaching with respect to the Law but also applies more widely: 'If salvation comes only in

---

[31] E. P. Sanders, *Paul and Palestinian Judaism: A Comparison of Patterns of Religion* (London: SCM Press, 1977), 485.

Christ, no one may follow any other way whatsoever'.[32] However, if this is right, then we can also begin to defend Luther, along with the other Reformers, as they applied the letter to the Galatians to the Roman church of their day. There is some irony here, of course, because many 'New Perspective' interpreters following in the steps of Sanders have argued that the Reformers woefully misapplied Galatians to soteriological issues when they should have been applying it to ecclesiological ones. This is because they suppose the main problem from Paul's point of view was that the Galatians were being persuaded to *turn to* a state where all the old boundaries between Jew and Gentile were re-erected. But if we relocate the main problem not on what the Galatians were being persuaded to *turn to*, rather on what they are being persuaded to *turn from*, then the picture changes significantly. Beginning with the pastoral perspective reminds us that the most dangerous characteristic of 'those of the works of the law' was that they were *severing people from Christ*. But that is also the dangerous characteristic of Pelagianism and semi-Pelegianism — and a whole host of other things too. So as we think about how this letter speaks into situations in the generations following the Galatian crisis, we do not have to demonstrate, assume or assert that

---

[32] Sanders, *Paul and Palestinian Judaism*, 519 Sanders is wrong, of course, to suggest Paul only properly argues from solution to plight, as in 'Man's plight is basically to be understood as the antithesis to the solution to it as Paul understood that solution' (Sanders, *Paul and Palestinian Judaism*, 497). Paul does argue from solution to plight: note especially 2:21, 'I do not nullify the grace of God, for if justification were through the law, then Christ died for no purpose.' If Christ's death was absolutely necessary (and of course it must have been), and took place to give justification, then *all* other proposed means of justification *must* be inadequate. However, I shall be arguing in section 4 that Paul *also* argues coherently from plight to solution in 3:8-14, even if some of the steps are only implicit.

'those of the works of the law' *were* actually proto-Pelagians or semi-Pelagians or 'legalists' of a particular kind in order to preach against Pelagians, semi-Pelagians or other kinds of 'legalists' through it. Such people may not be trying to sever Christians from Christ in *quite the same way* as Paul's opponents — but there are notable similarities and the end effect would be the same: death and curse. The exhortation is the same: 'let Christ be (re-)formed in you' (cf. 4:19). And in many ways we shall find the argument against these other forms of false teaching can proceed on largely the same lines as Paul's.

3.4. A pastoral 'way-in' to the argument in 3:8-14

The pastoral perspective therefore helps us to locate the main problem in Galatia as Paul saw it, and we have argued that it was that people were being persuaded to abandon Christ. We can respect Spurgeon's pastoral passion as he preached on Galatians 3:13, and with a little charity we can relate it to Paul's concerns. However, we would do better to centre our pastoral focus in preaching Paul more precisely where he did. Paul's anguish that the Galatians may be turning away from Christ crucified pervades the letter, and of course it sets the stage in chapter 3:

> 'O foolish Galatians! Who has bewitched you? It was before your eyes that Jesus Christ was publicly portrayed as crucified. [2] Let me ask you only this: Did you receive the Spirit by works of the law or by hearing with faith? [3] Are you so foolish? Having begun by the Spirit, are you now being perfected by the flesh? [4] Did you suffer so many things in vain — if indeed it was in vain?

The question is, as the argument continues: how will he persuade them to turn back?

4. Preaching Paul as Story-Teller

If the pastoral perspective helps us to locate the main problem from Paul's point of view (that the Galatians may be abandoning Christ crucified, of whom they heard and received through the work of the Spirit), then the main claim of this section is that it is the narrative perspective that will be especially helpful in tracing how he persuades them to turn back. This is what Paul says, picking things up at verse 5:

> [5] Does he who supplies the Spirit to you and works miracles among you do so by works of the law, or by hearing with faith — [6] just as Abraham 'believed God, and it was counted to him as righteousness'?

> [7] Know then that it is those of faith who are the sons of Abraham.[8] And the Scripture, foreseeing that God would justify the Gentiles by faith, preached the gospel beforehand to Abraham, saying, 'In you shall all the nations be blessed.' [9] So then, those who are of faith are blessed along with Abraham, the man of faith.

> [10] For all who rely on works of the law are under a curse; for it is written, 'Cursed be everyone who does not abide by all things written in the Book of the Law, and do them.' [11] Now it is evident that no one is justified before God by the law, for 'The righteous shall live by faith.' [12] But the law is not of faith, rather 'The one who does them shall live by them.' [13] Christ redeemed us from the curse of the law by becoming a curse for us — for it is written, 'Cursed is everyone who is hanged on a tree' — [14] so that in Christ Jesus the blessing of Abraham might come to the Gentiles, so that we might receive the promised Spirit through faith.

We shall be seeing that as Paul persuades the Galatians to turn back he is both alluding to a story and telling a story and, if that is so, then we shall want to follow Paul's example and preach as story-tellers. But *what* story is Paul alluding to as he throws out the six citations in Galatians 3:6-14? What story is he then telling, as he speaks into the Galatian situation? And how should the pastor today follow his example and tell the story as it corresponds to *his* situation?

We should not be under the illusion that this is going to be easy. Moisés Silva's excellent book on exegetical method,[33] which takes Galatians as a case-study, has an amusing introduction to some of the difficulties presented by these verses:

> The first thesis ... is that the Galatians received the Spirit through (the hearing of) faith, and this affirmation is supported by citing Gen. 15:6. Curiously, though, this OT passage says nothing about the Holy Spirit.
>
> Paul next, in Gal. 3:7 [and 3:9], states that the true children of Abraham are 'the ones of faith' and in support cites Gen. 12:3, ... although that passage says nothing about faith. ...
>
> Third, the apostle directs our attention in 3:10 to 'as many as are of the works of the law' and affirms that they are under a curse, a thesis supported by appeal to Deut. 27:26. ... On the face of it, Deut. 27:26 (which curses those who disobey the law) seems to state precisely the opposite point that Paul wants to make ...
>
> The fourth thesis (Gal. 3:11) ... is that through the law no one can be made right with (or considered righteous by) God, and the grounds for this denial is Hab. 2:4, a passage which says nothing about the law. ...[34]

Clearly, Paul has left a great deal unsaid, and is assuming

---

[33] Moisés Silva, *Interpreting Galatians: Explorations in Exegetical Method* (Grand Rapids, Michigan: Baker Academic, 2001).
[34] Silva, *Interpreting Galatians*, 220–21.

much common ground with his readers. Silva concludes: 'It is difficult not to be impressed, on the one hand, by the care and effectiveness with which these various themes have been interwoven and, on the other hand, by the glaring gaps in the argumentation'.[35]

The plan for the section is this: Our aim is first, to find and defend the *background story* to 3:1-14, what is sometimes called its 'narrative substructure'. This is the story Paul is implying, and is to an extent assuming his readers already know. The suggestion here is that this is what we need to do as a priority to understand the flow of thought. We shall then be in a much better position to reappraise how Paul is re-telling this story into the Galatian situation, and think through how a preacher-as-storyteller might re-tell that story today.

4.1.   Two controls

Whether it is possible to reconstruct the background story Paul has in mind is a moot point. There are dangers, certainly[36] — and a degree of speculation will be necessary.

---

[35] Silva, *Interpreting Galatians*, 221.
[36] Barry Matlock admits that he once dismissed the narrative approach to Paul as: 'What you do when the Pauline text doesn't actually say what you need it to (i.e. you read it in light of the *underlying narrative*)' (R. Barry Matlock, "The Arrow and the Web: Critical Reflections on a Narrative Approach to Paul," in *Narrative Dynamics in Paul: A Critical Assessment* [ed. Bruce W. Longenecker; Louisville, London: Westminster John Knox Press, 2002], 44). The ambivalence of some of the authors in this volume to the narrative approach to Paul seems to stem partly from the mixed results it has generated and partly from a reluctance to accept any story-telling element in Paul at all. Francis Watson goes so far as to say, '[...] with the exception of Galatians 1-2, Paul in his extant writings never actually tells a story' (Francis Watson, "Is There a Story in These Texts?" in *Narrative Dynamics in Paul: A Critical Assessment* [ed. Bruce W. Longenecker; Louisville, London:

To keep the speculation to a minimum, we shall be using two controls. The first is to employ Francis Watson's reminder that Paul is *interpreting* Scripture for the situation which pertains in the Galatian church.[37] We shall assume that he does so consistently. So the first control is:

Control 1. Does the implied background story 'fit' with what Paul is saying?

That is, is it consistent with, and does it make sense of, the story he speaks into the Galatian situation, so that it flows coherently?

The second control is to assume that the background story will be consistent with a reading of the Scriptural narrative in its entirety and 'on its own terms' (i.e. independently of Paul). So the second control is:

Control 2. Does the implied background story 'fit' with the narrative of the Scriptures on their own terms?

That is, when we compare an independent reading of the Scriptures to the background story, do they contradict? This will be hard to establish, of course, but this control will at least encourage us to make an effort to defend this 'independent reading' exegetically.

Westminster John Knox Press, 2002], 239). I shall be suggesting Galatians 3:8-14 as a counter-example.
[37]Francis Watson, *Paul and the Hermeneutics of Faith* (London, New York: T & T Clark International, 2004), passim.

We can picture these controls like this:

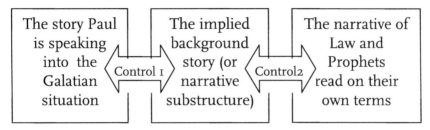

The story Paul is speaking into the Galatian situation		The implied background story (or narrative substructure)		The narrative of Law and Prophets read on their own terms
	Control 1		Control 2	

I shall take these two controls as giving necessary conditions for the 'true' background story or narrative substructure underlying what Paul is saying. They may not be sufficient to pin it down precisely.[38] However, we shall find these are strong enough to help shape what we conclude and to exclude some important alternatives.

4.2.   *Some previous attempts*

Before we begin on our own attempt, it is worth noting that the search for the 'narrative substructure' to these verses in Galatians 3 is not a new one. There is even an *implied* 'narrative substructure' in the traditional Protestant reading[39] of these verses which maintains that Paul is implying a 'missing premise' as he quotes Deut. 27:26: all are disobedient and do not do what the law demands. This does well under the first of our controls. This is not surprising, since it comes from assuming Paul is arguing according to a simple syllogism: the 'missing premise' is what makes the logic flow. If all are disobedient, then anyone seeking to do the law will fail and trigger the curse of Deut. 27:26. If all are disobedient, then the set of people finding life according to

---

[38] I do not know how one could prove a set of conditions *sufficient* to do this.
[39] I shall call this 'the traditional reading' from now on.

Lev. 18:5 is empty (and always has been). The grounds for justification must lie somewhere else, by faith, as in Hab. 2:4. It makes some sense of Paul's argument.

However, it does much less well under the second control *if* it is taken to imply that when Moses spoke the words of Deut. 27:26 to the Israelites on the borders of the Promised Land he meant that unless the whole law were kept *perfectly* by all the people *in every detail*, the covenant curses would be triggered. Deuteronomy simply does not read this way.[40] However, having said that, I shall be defending a *qualified* version of the 'missing premise' in what follows. (More on this later.)

Dissatisfaction with the traditional reading has been a hallmark of 'New Perspective' approaches to Galatians 3:6-14, but the results have been extremely varied. Richard Hays, for example, is engaged in a search for the narrative substructure of Galatians to defend his thesis that 'faith' in Galatians always refers to the faithfulness of Christ rather than the faith

---

[40] Indeed, we are told in Deuteronomy the exact conditions under which the covenant curses will be triggered some time in the future. While it is true that the triggering of the curses shall be associated with a failure to be 'careful to do all his commandments' (e.g. Deut. 28:15), this is not like the pedantic legalism of Portia saying to Shylock in *The Merchant of Venice* that if, when he cuts his pound of flesh, it differs from a pound 'in the estimation of a hair', then 'thou diest and all thy goods are confiscate' (Act 4, Scene 1). Rather, a failure to be 'careful to do all God's commandments' is expressive of a deeper problem: a problem of the 'heart' (Deut. 29:4, 19). God says that if (when) the curses are triggered, it will be 'because you have forsaken me' (Deut 28:20). The nations will say, when God's people are sent into exile, it was 'because they abandoned the covenant of the LORD ... and served other gods and worshipped them' (Deut 29:25-28). And this is borne out in actual history as we read on. Israel is not sent into exile over some minor deviation from perfection — because, say, someone happened to trip up by wearing cloth of wool and linen mixed together (cf. Deut. 22:11). Israel is sent into exile because of wholesale national apostasy and spiritual adultery.

of the believer.[41] James Dunn builds a background story which focuses on the nationalistic boundary markers of the Law in tension with the promise of blessing to the nations.[42] Tom Wright is engaged in a similar search in the chapter 'Curse and Covenant: Galatians 3:10-14' in his book *The Climax of the Covenant*.[43] In this reconstruction, there is a set sequence of events necessary in the story of Israel before God's blessing can pass to the Gentiles. Because Israel is the set means by which this blessing will propagate, she must *truly* return from exile before it can happen. By taking the exilic curses upon himself, Jesus provides the 'missing link,' so to speak. The 'us' in 3:13 is thus 'us Jews still in exile'. (We shall be pursuing below a much more straightforward reason why the cross leads to the blessing of Abraham coming to the Gentiles.)

4.3.   An Alternative Background Story

Even if we find it hard to agree entirely with the various 'New Perspective' reconstructions, let us suppose that Paul *is* alluding to a story in 3:6-14, referenced by his citations from the Scriptures. If that is correct, then it is telling in itself. It suggests that one of the big errors of his opponents has been to fail to take the wider story into consideration. They have focussed on one part of the story, they have dangerously divorced that part from its context, and have made it the

---

[41] Richard B. Hays, *The Faith of Jesus Christ: The Narrative Substructure of Galatians 3:1–4:11* (SBL Dissertation Series 56; Chico, California: Scholar's Press, 1983).

[42] James D. G. Dunn, *Jesus, Paul and the Law: Studies in Mark and Galatians* (London: SPCK, 1990), 215–41.

[43] N. T. Wright, *The Climax of the Covenant: Christ and the Law in Pauline Theology* (Minneapolis: Fortress Press, 1993), 137–56.

static, atemporal centre of everything. What I think we shall see is that while Paul is not concerned to tell every detail of the wider story with the support of these citations, what he does do is tell the story in such a way that highlights the fact if you line up with Israel-before-Christ (i.e. Israel 'under the law') then you are lining up with *failed* Israel, leaving you likewise under God's curse. That is the context in which verse 13 makes such a strong pastoral impact.

What I am about to argue is that the background story Paul has in mind (and, to an extent, expects to share with his readers) is that which begins with the curse of death, progresses through Abraham to Sinai, but is complicated and left unresolved by the failure of Israel. We shall see then that this background story greatly affects what these citations now mean when applied to the situation in Galatia compared to what they would have meant to their first hearers. We shall also see the advantages of a slightly different form of perspectival thinking as we do so (the 'speech-act' perspectivalism of section 2.1 above).

4.3.1. *The background story beginning with the curse of death.*

Take the first two of Paul's citations here: in verse 6, from Genesis 15:6, [Abraham[44]] 'believed God, and it was counted to him as righteousness'; and in verse 8, from Genesis 12:3, 'In you shall all the nations be blessed.' The key to untangling the web of implicit connections Paul makes in 3:1-9 between the Spirit, blessing, and justification must surely build around his interpretation of these verses. However, we shall only begin to see those connections, and thereby satisfy

---

[44] I shall follow Paul's convention in always using the name 'Abraham' even when referring to events which took place before his renaming.

our first control, if we take the background story Paul is implying in his citation of those verses lies one in which the blessing (of life) promised through Abraham is always relative to the curse (of death) that entered the world through Adam. But that background story is actually quite consistent with the promises to Abraham in Gen. 12:1-3 read on their own terms (which is our second control).

Indeed, what we find when we turn to the promises of two-stage blessing to Abraham (first for the nation, Gen. 12:2; then for all the families of the earth, Gen. 12:3) is that they only have the dramatic impact the author intends when they are taken in contrast to the (global) problem of curse/death brought into the world by Adam which has filled the dark pages of Genesis 1-11. It may even be that the author of Genesis is emphasising this connection by using the word 'blessing' five times in these two verses, to contrast with the five occurrences of 'curse' in Genesis 1-11.

To claim that the background story begins with Adam might sound implausible at first since, unlike Romans, Galatians contains not a single direct mention of Adam.[45]

---

[45] Although 3:8, 'neither male nor female' could be an allusion to Gen 1:27. A comparison with Romans is instructive in that in his longer discussion Paul does make the link back to Adam more explicit. Douglas Moo comments on Rom 5:12-21: 'Israel and the law figure as part of a continuous story from Adam to Christ, [...] Paul treats the law in vv.12-21 as an aside in the story he is telling' (Douglas J. Moo, "Israel and the Law in Romans 5–11: Interaction with the New Perspective," in *Justification and Variegated Nomism: Volume 2 – the Paradoxes of Paul* [eds D.A. Carson, et al.; Grand Rapids, Michigan: Baker Academic, 2004], 195). Furthermore, the conclusions Moo reaches from Romans fit very well with the conclusions we shall reach from Galatians below. Paul's criticism of the law focuses 'on its failure to deliver sinful Jews from the nexus of sin and death — a criticism that extends ultimately to all human beings, who find their best representation in the Jewish people' (Moo, "Israel and the Law," 216).

However, I would like to suggest that this background in Adam is implicit (Paul might even say, 'is evident'!) every time he mentions Abraham.

4.3.2. *Genesis 12:3 and 15:6 read perspectivally.*

So notice how Paul is reading and using these citations. He is reading them *perspectivally*. As we saw in section 2.1 one way of thinking perspectivally about a text of Scripture is 'speech-act' perspectivalism. We distinguish between its verbal content, the situation in which it is spoken, and the people to whom it is spoken. The words 'In you shall all the nations be blessed' were spoken to Abraham in an apparently hopeless historical context of global curse and death. But Paul is now using them in a new context, for a new set of people. In these new circumstances there is still global curse and death, but things have progressed: Christ has been crucified and *Gentiles* have received the Spirit! (More precisely: Gentiles have heard with faith Jesus Christ portrayed as crucified and have thereby received the Spirit, 3:1-5.) In these new circumstances, the words say to the Galatians, '*You* have been blessed, just as God promised.' And the words '[Abraham] believed God, and it was credited to him as righteousness' say to the Galatians, '*You* (if you are those of faith) are the sons of Abraham, justified by your *faith,* just as he was'.[46]

---

[46] Notice that, unlike Hays, *The Faith of Jesus Christ*, 196–203, we have made no reference in the discussion so far to Christ's faithfulness. To bring in Christ too early in 3:6-14 would spoil the story. Paul is waiting to bring in Christ climatically in verse 13.

4.3.3. *The background story progressing from Adam, through Abraham, to Israel*

The second claim I wish to defend is that Paul assumes a strong connection between Adam and Israel, and a parallel between the failure of Adam and the failure and apostasy of Israel. This is so strong that what happens to Israel in his background story *to some extent* mirrors[47] what happened to Adam. This will help to explain how Paul can move so freely in his argument from Abraham, who stands against the global backdrop of the curse of death, to the curse *of the Law* in verses 10-13. Again, this may sound implausible, since (again, unlike Romans) Galatians contains only one mention of Israel,[48] and no *direct* reference to her failure, nor to the exile which followed. However, I would like to suggest that this background is implicit (again, Paul might say, 'is evident') whenever Paul cites the conditional statements of the Sinai covenant which were originally addressed to Israel and now, post-exile, evoke her failure.

Think first about the parallels between the conditional statements of the Sinai covenant (which Paul cites here from Deut. 27:26 and Lev. 18:5) and the conditional statement given to Adam in Gen. 2:16-17. They both have the form, 'If you transgress my boundaries, you will be cursed/die.' As she

---

[47] I am hoping that 'to some extent' staves off a discussion of exactly *how* close. There is a danger here of raising too many issues to deal with all at once. I shall try to make it clear how far we need to take the parallel to make sense of Paul's argument.

[48] The 'Israel of God' in 6:16. The expression is debated, but Paul seems to be making a clear distinction between this body and pre-Christ, failed Israel. Dunn may be right here, saying this is 'Israel understood in terms of the promise to Abraham (and Jacob/Israel)... *not* excluding Jews, but as *including* Gentile believers', Dunn, James D. G., *A Commentary of the Epistle to the Galatians* (Black's New Testament Commentaries; London: A&C Black, 1993), 345.

hears those conditions, and especially as she begins to experience the blessing, she stands rather as Adam did in the blessing of the garden in Genesis 2 — at least to some extent. Israel *should* have been (in the sense that she was commanded to be) a new Adam. Indeed, it is striking that for Israel the conditionals are stated positively, as in Deut 28:1-6 and Lev 18:5, for example, and have the form 'Obey and you will be blessed/live'. It is as if God wishes to stress the possibility (in *some* sense[49]) of walking with him — he is saying, 'You can do it' (Deut. 30:14). Or, at least, you *should* be able to do it.

Think secondly about the parallels between Israel's failure and Adam's failure. The story of Israel proceeds badly from here, as predicted. Loving, trusting, faith-empowered obedience *should* have been possible, but for the nation as a whole it proved not to be. Let us fast-forward now to Israel at

---

[49] Taken as a whole, Moses seems to be saying in Deuteronomy that walking with God will be possible for Israel in one sense (no one is stopping them, and God is providing many privileges to help them), but it will prove impossible in another (their hearts will bring failure in the end). What it means for something to be 'possible' is a complex issue in philosophy and we do not wish to get too side-tracked here by the metaphysics of modality. However, Jonathan Edwards would have said that walking with God was a *natural* possibility for Israel while remaining a *moral* impossibility (Jonathan Edwards, *Freedom of the Will* [ed. P Ramsey; The Works of Jonathan Edwards, Vol. 1; New Haven and London: Yale University Press, 1985; first published 1754]). This should *not* be taken as saying Israel had no sinful nature: 'We are said to be *naturally* unable to do a thing, when we can't do it when we [want to]' ... '*Moral inability* consists... either in the want of inclination; or the strength of a contrary inclination; or want of sufficient motives in view...' (p.159). That is, if something is naturally possible, nothing is stopping you from doing it, although you may prove morally incapable of doing it. Or, if all that seems contrived, we can think of Moses arguing like this: 1) This is the way humans were created to be; 2) you are human; 3) therefore it is natural for you to be this way, and you should be. We might add: *especially* you, chosen by God. (Thanks to Peter Bolt for this observation.)

the point of apostasy. Apostasy is not *merely* disobedience, of course (although it will inevitably express itself in disobedience); apostasy is an act of utterly turning one's back on God — his blessing, his mercy and his promises. It places Israel back to square one; effectively, back in the garden, at the point when Adam too was spurning the blessing of God. And then, consequently, 'out of the garden', in exile. Israel under God's curse has so sunk back into the morass of Adamic humanity as to be indistinguishable from it. It may no longer even be appropriate to call her 'Israel' any more.[50] And here is the point we wished to establish: now it becomes clearer than ever that dealing with the 'curse of the Law' will *also* deal with the curse of death which entered the world through Adam.

The biblical parallels between Adam and apostate Israel, between garden and Land, between the expulsion of Genesis 3 and the exile, are too striking to miss. What we are beginning to see is that one way of unpicking the difficulties in 3:1-14 is to suppose that Paul moves between them freely. What makes them parallel? Marginalising the promise, spurning the blessing, casting it to one side. This was the error of apostate Israel. And Paul is greatly afraid that the Galatians are about to repeat their mistake.

4.3.4. *Deut. 27:26 and Lev. 18:5 read perspectivally.*

So again it is helpful to notice that Paul is reading and using these citations perspectivally. Take Paul's citation, in verse 10, from Deut. 27:26,

'Cursed be everyone who does not abide by all things

---

[50] Which may be why Paul steers clear of that name in Galatians.

written in the Book of the Law, and do them.'

As Moses spoke these words to God's people on the brink of the Promised Land, these represented the second of two possible paths. The first was the path of covenant faithfulness expressed in actual obedience, leading to life. This second path was the path to curse and death. Moses knows the nation will choose this second path. But there is no good reason, apart from their hardness of heart, why they shouldn't choose the first.

After the failure of Israel and the triggering of these curses, the words take on a somewhat different flavour. They stand as an indictment against the nation in which *every* deviation from the things written in the Book of the Law is evidence for the prosecution. This is the sense in which they should speak to the Galatians.

It is similar with Paul's citation, in verse 12, from Lev. 18:5: 'The one who does them shall live by them.' Read in original context (both historical and literary) Lev. 18:5 is part of a call to act out what it means to be redeemed from Egypt and separated from the Canaanites. As Joel Willitts helpfully puts it, it 'offers forth the potential for which YHWH entered into the covenant with Israel, that they might live...'[51]

But as Israel fails, Lev. 18:5 comes back to haunt them. This was word of the Lord to Ezekiel as elders of Israel come to enquire of him:

> ...the children rebelled against me. They did not walk in my statutes and were not careful to obey my rules, by which, if a person does them, he shall live by them... (Ez. 20:21; cf.

---

[51] Joel Willits, "Context Matters: Paul's Use of Leviticus 18:5 in Galatians 3:12," *Tyndale Bulletin* 54, no. 2 (2003): 111.

20:11, 13 and Neh. 9:29.)

As Willits says of the *later* use of Lev. 18:5: '...but now ironically, in the light of Israel's history, it comes to signify the *unrealised purpose* of the covenant within redemptive history... the squandering of the *potential* of the covenant relationship'.[52]

So where does this leave us? Well, it is true as an abstract and ahistorical statement that 'all are disobedient and do not do (perfectly) what the law demands' (the 'missing premise' under the traditional reading). But Paul is saying something like that but much *stronger*. He is saying, 'Even under the gracious provisions of the Mosaic economy, the hearts of men were so adulterous that they brought curse on themselves, as you well know. You will fare no better.' In the end, this is much more in keeping with the Reformed essentials that readers of *Latimer Studies* wish to be reminded of. Notice that although the traditional reading may allude to the depravity of mankind, it is actually optional to the argument. Mankind could be *near-perfect* and the logic would still follow through! Paul, on the other hand, wants to *emphasise* the depravity of mankind, and to magnify the grace of God in the redeeming, substitutionary death of Jesus, thereby exposing the culpable foolishness of turning to something else.

4.3.5. *Summary.*

Israel failed just as Adam failed. They could have had life and blessing, but they spurned it, and chose death and exile. The conditionals of the Sinai covenant stand as an indictment. To

---

[52] Willits, "Context Matters," 113–14.

become like Israel, to become one of 'those of the law', is therefore to embrace death.

4.4. *Galatians 3:8-14 revisited as story*

We are now in a position to revisit Galatians 3:8-14 and trace Paul's argument. Paul's method of argument is much discussed, and much has been said about how he is and is not using the tools of Classical Rhetoric.[53] But it may well be that Paul is not so much giving us a formal argument but rather telling us a story.

It has often been noticed that 3:8-14 are 'palistrophic'.[54] That is, there is a concentric structure here. At the centre, the keyword 'life' connects verses 11 and 12. Moving out from the centre, Paul has departed from the LXX in his citation of Deut. 21:23 so that the keyword 'curse' connects verses 10 and 13. Finally, the keyword 'blessing' connects verses 8-9 to verse 14. But exegetes do not seem to have known quite what to do with this. However, elsewhere in the Bible palistrophes are used as means of structuring stories — one thinks especially of the great cycles in Genesis and the court-intrigues in Daniel. If that is true here, then the structure it gives to Paul's story happens to be like that of a five-act play, a scheme of rising and falling action roughly corresponding to what is

---

[53] Enthusiasts include G. Walter Hansen, *Abraham in Galatians: Epistolary and Rhetorical Contexts* (Journal for the Study of the New Testament Supplement Series 29; Sheffield: JSOT Press, 1989) and D. Francois Tolmie, *Persuading the Galatians: A Text-Centred Rhetorical Analysis of a Pauline Letter* (Wissenschaftliche Untersuchungen Zum Neuen Testament. 2 Reihe. 190; Tübingen: Mohr Siebeck, 2005). For a skeptic, see Philip H. Kern, *Rhetoric and Galatians: Assessing an Approach to Paul's Epistle* (Society for New Testament Studies Monograph Series 101; Cambridge: Cambridge University Press, 1998).
[54] e.g. Silva, Interpreting Galatians, 91.

sometimes known as 'Freytag's Pyramid'.[55] Verses 8-9
provide the introduction, *setting the stage*. Verse 10 begins
the *rising action* and introduces a *complication* in the form of
an antagonist: the 'works of the law' group. This results in
(verses 11-12) the central *conflict* between the protagonists,
'those of faith', and the antagonists, 'those of works of law'.
This is decided (by Christ crucified) in the *climax,* verse 13.
Finally, we have the *dénouement* or conclusion, verse 14.

Let's see how this might work out in more detail:

4.4.1. *Setting the stage: where the Galatians were and still should be.*

Verses 8-9:

> ... the Scripture, foreseeing that God would justify the
> Gentiles by faith, preached the gospel beforehand to
> Abraham, saying, 'In you shall all the nations be blessed.'
> So then, *those who are of faith* are blessed along with
> Abraham, the man of faith. For...

Of course, the stage-setting begins earlier than this. Paul has
been reminding the Galatians that they received the Spirit by
hearing news of Christ crucified by faith (3:1-5). This has
aligned them with Abraham (3:6-7): it is those who are 'of
faith' who are the sons of Abraham. Here, Paul concludes the
stage-setting by saying they have been justified and blessed,
just as promised.

It is as if Paul is saying, '*You* (if you are those of faith)
are the sons of Abraham, justified by your *faith,* just as he

---

[55] After the analysis of plays by the nineteenth century critic Gustav Freytag. See
M.H. Abrams, *A Glossary of Literary Terms (5th Ed.)* (New York: Holt, Rinehart,
and Winston, 1988), 141.

was. *You* have been blessed, just as God promised. These are the privileges of being "of faith", which you had!'

4.4.2. *The complication (rising action): the danger of curse.*

Verse 10:

> For *those of works of law* [my trans] are under a curse, for it is written, 'Cursed be everyone who does not abide by all the things written in the book of the Law, and do them.'

This is the nightmare story Paul begins to take the Galatians through. The happy state of blessing is now under threat of curse. Antagonists have appeared, dangerous because of the curse they carry — which is the same curse as failed-Israel before Christ, who stand indicted by the law.

It is as if Paul is saying, 'You want to know why you should hold on to that blessing? You ask, "*What if* there was a better way?" What if you were in the "works of law" group, for example? Let us run that story and see what happens. Let me tell you: if that were the story, you would be at the same dead end as those to whom the law was given: under curse of law and curse of death...'

4.4.3. *The central conflict: life by faith versus the 'life' some other way.*

Verses 11-12:

> Now it is evident that no one is justified before God by the law, for 'The righteous shall live by faith.' But the law is not of faith, rather 'The one who does them shall live by them.'

Like Moses, Paul is now setting before the Galatians life and death. Life has always, can only, come from faith. What the 'works of law' party are offering is something else, however.

It is as if Paul is saying, 'Come, let's turn this sorry

tale around. You should already know that the way to life (confirmed by justification) is the way of faith, because God's people have already had to face up to that as things fell around them at the time of Habakkuk (when the law was paralysed and justice never went forth — Hab. 1:4). The only solution is to "live by faith". But to focus on the law in the manner of the "works of the law" party is not "of faith" — it is not depending on God's provision of life at all. That's burying your head in the sand and pretending Israel never failed. It looks attractive: it is packed with the *potential* of the Mosaic covenant. But don't you know that potential was unrealised? "The one who does them shall live by them" is no longer a slogan of hope, but a prophetic indictment!'

4.4.4. *The climax: curse defeated by the redeeming, substitutionary death of Christ.*

Verse 13:

> Christ redeemed us from the curse of the Law by becoming a curse for us — for it is written, 'Cursed is everyone who is hanged on a tree' —

Now we can begin to understand the asyndeton in this verse. This is Paul's trump card, put down in a flourish, and the climax which brings the nightmare to a welcome end.

It is as if he is saying, 'That state which you are in danger of slipping back into, that state in which you and I once were... well, Christ has redeemed us from it! He redeemed us by becoming a curse *for* us.[56] The depravity and

---

[56] Paul is taking it as obvious from Deut. 21:23 that a crucified person is a person 'hung on a tree' and thereby under God's curse. Why would the Christ do that? To redeem others from a *more general* curse, which we are arguing here to be the curse of sin and death. cf. Martyn, 'Christ's embodiment of the Law's curse was

hopelessness of that state was brought into sharp focus by the failure of Israel and the curse of the Law. In that we Jews sank back to your level. So when Christ redeems *us Jews*, he redeems *us all...*' (which leads to the dénouement...)

4.4.5. *The dénouement: the victory of blessing restored.*

Verse 14

> ...so that in Christ Jesus blessing might come to the Gentiles, so that we might receive the promised Spirit by faith.

Because of Christ, our story reaches a happy ending. Because of Christ, we return to the state we began with: Gentiles like the Galatians receiving blessing; those 'of faith' receiving the Spirit. The plight they have been rescued from was the universal, global curse of death, which came into particularly acute focus in failed-Israel under the curse of the Law. The solution was the redemptive, substitutionary death of Christ on the cross. By dealing with the plight at its most fundamental, accentuated level, this then paved the way for the blessing of Abraham to go to the nations.

And it as if Paul is saying, 'Why would you want to give *that* away?'

4.5. Re-telling the story today

So Paul's basic method is to keep people devoted to Christ by running them through the nightmare story of where they

---

the act in which the Law was robbed of its *universal* power to curse' (emphasis added, Martyn, *Galatians*, 321). We might also add, 'It is hard to imagine a plainer statement of the doctrine of penal substitution' (Jeffery, et al., *Pierced for Our Transgressions*, 89).

would stand with respect to God were they to abandon Christ for something else. And this helps them to refocus on the cross, because the only way the story can have a happy ending (with even Gentiles like themselves blessed!) is through the redeeming, substitutionary work of Christ.

The preacher today will want to tell again the story Paul told the Galatians. But he will also want to run his listeners through the nightmare story of where they would stand with respect to God were they to abandon Christ in ways that are different to the Galatians, but which happen to seem attractive at that moment. In principle, we could do this with *any* temptation to abandon Christ for something else. However, we shall get a closer fit to Galatians 3:6-14 if we focus on examples where the 'something else', like joining 'those of the works of the law', *claims* to be especially honouring to God, but in reality is not. (I shall return with some suggestions in the conclusion.)

We can also make the following points:

First, we can say: At least the Galatians were being fooled by something that *looked* good. They were being offered something which seemed (with a little crafty sales spin) to have God's seal of approval in the Scriptures. And yet it was still foolish. How much more is it foolish to abandon Christ for *this* thing (whatever it is)!

We can also say: Don't you know how weak your hearts are? Listen again as Paul reminds you of the failure of Israel. The human heart is so weak it fails even when people are smothered by God's kindness. Doesn't that make you want to cling to the climactic blessing of God in Christ all the more tightly?

But no doubt all of this will provoke one or two questions...

5. Preaching Paul as Sage

The pastoral perspective has suggested the main problem facing Paul was that the Galatians were in danger of abandoning Christ. The narrative perspective has helped us to understand how in 3:8-14 especially Paul is exposing the foolishness of that and persuading them to turn back. Finally, we come to the systematic perspective.

And let me begin by claiming that a good pastor will not be able to avoid thinking about his preaching from a systematic perspective. Richard Baxter makes this point:

> ...if you examine, you will find that most of the preaching recorded in the New Testament, was by conference, and frequently interlocutory, and that with one or two, fewer or more, as opportunity served. Thus Christ himself did most commonly preach.[57]

Baxter is using the term 'preaching' quite broadly, to cover dialogue, reasoning and discourse in the New Testament. Even so, what he says helps to prick the pretence that 'proper' preaching is a rigidly one-way monologue from preacher to congregation. It may well be that the sustained and uninterrupted monologue that has become the norm in 'Western' culture today only became so under the nineteenth century fashion for strict public decorum. Elsewhere it seems to be much more common for speakers to stop to deal with interruptions, questions or objections.

And it is striking that even in a *letter,* which you might have thought would inevitably be a one-way monologue, we

---

[57] Richard Baxter, *The Reformed Pastor* (reprint, 1656; Edinburgh: Banner of Truth, 1974), 228.

find Paul effectively engaging in dialogue. There is some debate in the literature about this, but we do not need to have mastered that debate to see that Paul is constantly raising and answering questions in his letter, as if to anticipate the concerns and confusions of his recipients. Some obvious examples are in 2:17; 3:19 and 3:21.

I want to make the claim that this *is* systematic theology in action. Systematic theology is born out of conversation, controversy and debate. It is 'elenctic' (i.e. aimed at *convicting* antagonists concerning the truth) as anyone who has read Turretin will already know.[58] And part of the role of the pastor in preaching (whether we take 'preaching' in a narrow or a broad sense) is to *answer questions:* questions that are put to him, questions he anticipates, questions he raises himself. It is as he answers those questions that he will be helping his questioners (and himself!) to bring together, integrate and systematise what God has been saying through the Scriptures, so that it can be seen as the coherent package it truly is.

5.1. How does Galatians 3:8-14 (and v.13 in particular) contribute to the *concept* of redemption?

This is one of the main systematic questions raised by what we have looked at. This is what we shall need to answer to demonstrate the coherency of the Scriptural teaching on redemption. Let us begin with an answer supplied by John Murray:

'Christ hath redeemed us from the curse of the law, being

---

[58] Francis Turretin, *Institutes of Elenctic Theology* (trans. George Musgrave Giger; ed. James T. Dennison; Phillipsburg, N.J.: P&R Publishing, 1992-c1997).

made a curse for us' (Gal. 3:13). The curse of the law is its penal sanction. [...] It is from this curse that Christ has purchased his people and the price of the purchase was that he himself became a curse. [...] That was the price paid for this redemption and the liberty secured for the beneficiaries is that there is no more curse.[59]

Notice how Murray instinctively assumes that the redemption secured by Christ in this verse has a global scope, and that he has effectively universalised the law, without pausing to justify himself. However, our analysis from a narrative perspective helps us to confirm this instinct (broadly, at least), to fill in the gaps in reasoning somewhat, and to provide a little more depth. Despite all its privileges, Israel under the curse of the Mosaic law had so sunk back into the morass of Adamic humanity as to be indistinguishable from it. The slavery of failed-Israel became indistinguishable from the slavery of the Gentile sinner (cf. 4:3, 9). By taking upon himself the curse *of the law* Christ is then dealing with plight of *all humanity* at its most fundamental, accentuated level, a redemption which paved the way for the blessing of Abraham to go to the nations.

There is no doubt more we could say, and there are subtleties in moving from the use of a particular word to a general systematic concept.[60] However, the preacher of Paul needs at least to be aware that as he expounds the various Scriptural data on 'redemption' there will be building in the minds of his hearers a composite picture of 'redemption'

---

[59] John Murray, *Redemption Accomplished and Applied* (Grand Rapids: Eerdmans, 1955), 44.
[60] As brought to the attention of biblical scholars by James Barr, *The Semantics of Biblical Language* (Oxford: Oxford University Press, 1961). See also Poythress, *Symphonic Theology*, especially pp.74–79.

(whether it is catalogued under that term or not). It is incumbent upon him to do his best to make sure that picture makes sense.

5.2. Question time

Thinking about redemption may be one of the 'main' systematic questions facing the preacher of 3:13. However, we cannot rely on our hearers asking the main or most obvious questions! Like Paul, we can build this question-answer format into our preaching, as we anticipate objections, but we are unlikely to anticipate them all. How wonderful it would be if our meetings were also so relaxed as to allow the occasional interruption! I suspect this may be too counter-cultural for 'Westerners'. In any case, many meetings are simply too large for this to be practicable. The alternative is to designate a separate question and answer session after the sermon has been given. This is becoming more common, and can work very well indeed.

Experience shows that the questions people ask can be extremely varied and may wander considerably from the central point a preacher is trying to make. What follows are a fairly random selection of questions to illustrate this.

5.2.1. So let me get this straight: what exactly does it mean to be 'of those of works of law'?

As I said earlier, it may well be God's good providence that Paul holds back from answering this question completely. Frustrating, perhaps, and it *has* caused some confusion, to be sure! But the key thing to pick up from Galatians is the folly of abandoning Christ, rather than feeling we must go away with a *complete* picture of how Christ was being abandoned in this particular instance.

However, the story we told in the previous section suggests that what the 'works of law' party were doing was going back (or holding on) to the pre-Christ orientation to the law of failed-Israel. This attitude marginalised Christ and implied he need not have died (see especially 2:21). The insistence on circumcision 'dates' this attitude to the law as pre-Christ or Christ-denying, in that it denies the work of Christ in bringing the blessing of Abraham to the uncircumcised nations.

Were they legalists? *Yes,* in that they were pushing aside the salvation graciously offered by God in Christ and were therefore *in some sense* 'going it alone'. *Not necessarily,* in that we need not suppose they thought their obedience to the law was *earning* them favour from an ungracious God. But the argument about whether Paul is directly attacking legalism is extremely messy, and nobody seems to be able to agree on terms.[61] In the end, we might wonder how fruitful this argument is. After all, as has already been said, Paul is *indirectly* attacking all forms of legalism, since all forms of legalism (if they mean anything substantial at all) will involve abandoning Christ.

5.2.2. *What does it mean to be 'justified'?*

I shall limit myself to one brief observation, which is to note that in 3:11-12 'to be justified before God' is strongly connected to *life* (living in relationship with God: either 'by

---

[61] John Piper quotes a personal email from Matt Perman: 'When I read E. P. Sanders, what stood out to me was that legalism was in almost every quote that he gave from Judaism in his attempt to prove it was not legalistic. It became clear to me that Sanders doesn't seem to know what legalism is' (Piper, *The Future of Justification*, 152, n.14).

faith' or 'by the law'). In other words, the 'vertical' dimension between God and the one justified seems to be dominant. That said, what happens in the vertical dimension certainly has automatic 'horizontal' ramifications. To be justified, to have life from God, to be blessed by God, is also to be 'a son of Abraham' (3:7), included in the covenant.

This welding of the soteriological and social aspects of justification is nicely expressed by Michael Bird: 'Paul articulates an understanding of justification that accentuates the facets of *divine vindication* and *covenant inclusion:* God creates a new people, with a new status, in a new covenant, in the wake of the new age'.[62]

5.2.3.   *So why then the law?*

This is a question Paul anticipates himself. 'It was added because of transgressions...' says Paul (3:19a). At first glance this looks like it just muddies the water! But actually, it supports what we have been saying. The question is something like: once we have seen the failure of the human heart in the cursing and exile of Israel, and once we have seen the necessity of *faith*—of depending on God's solution—we are bound to ask: looking back, why then the law? *In the end,* what purpose did it serve in the time before Christ?

Well, we have already said it. The curse of the law applied to failed-Israel has *exposed* the failure of the human heart. *Human transgression* has been magnified for all to see, '...until the offspring has come to whom the promise had been made' (3:19b). The law is therefore not opposed to the

---

[62] Bird, *The Saving Righteousness of God,* 152–53.

promise (3:21ff).

5.2.4. *So are you saying that anyone who fails to depend on God's redemption from the curse of the law is under a curse?* ....

Yes.

5.2.5. *So how then may I be saved?*

Let's leave the last word to Spurgeon:

> But to close: here I have one who is saying, 'What must I do to be saved, for I feel myself condemned?' [...] Sinner! it is no use for thee to try and save yourself; but to believe in Christ is the only way of salvation; and that is, throwing self behind your back, and putting Christ right before thee. [...] to believe is to fall flat down upon the promise and there to lie.[63]

6.   Conclusion

We have been thinking about an *approach* to preaching. I have not given a homiletical method, like Spurgeon's ubiquitous, 'State the point, explain it, illustrate it and apply it.' Rather, I have suggested that we face up to our limitations and inability to see everything important all at once, and self-consciously to approach the task of preaching from three perspectives. The ones I have suggested are: the *pastoral* perspective, thinking about the well-being of our listeners, the *narrative* perspective, thinking about God's story of

---

[63] Spurgeon, "The Curse Removed."

redemption, big-scale and small, and the *systematic* perspective, asking and answering questions to clarify what we have said and check that it all fits together.

Turning to Galatians 3:8-14, we found that the pastoral perspective helped us see Paul's central anguish that people he loved were abandoning Christ (in this case, by following 'those of works of law'). The narrative perspective helped us to think though the big background story of redemption Paul has in mind, and how he is re-telling that story to bring his listeners back to Christ. Having set the scene by reminding the Galatians of the international blessing they were part of, he runs them through the nightmare story of where they would stand before God were they to abandon Christ for the 'works of law' party: a story that *only* has a happy ending, with international blessing restored, because of the redemptive, substitutionary death of Christ. We said this technique could work well with other examples of people tempted to abandon Christ in similar ways (more on that in a moment). Finally, the systematic perspective helped us to check that we were able to give some sort of coherent answers to questions raised by what we have said.

I am not pretending that any of this will make a noticeable contribution to the debate about the 'New Perspective'. Still, it seems to me that Reformed exegetes tend to be weak on the narrative perspective, New Perspective exegetes tend to be weak on the systematic perspective (which is one reason why the stories they tell are so varied), and everyone is weak on the pastoral perspective! A more balanced approach could be a constructive way forward.

I said that we would return to the pastoral perspective in the conclusion. Let me say first that part of my aim has been to rescue the preaching of Paul from those specialists who want to take its relevance away from us. We simply do not have to be experts in the writings of Second Temple Judaism, or experts in *anything* much, to see that Paul's primary pastoral anguish is seeing his friends turning away from an exclusive dependency on Christ. The historical debate on what exactly the 'works of law' party believed and were insisting on will no doubt simmer on, but the key thing is: it was not Christ. And the arguments Paul uses against them, the stories he tells, can also be used against other examples of abandoning Christ.

I said in section 4 that in principle, we could do this with *any* temptation to abandon Christ for something else. However, we shall get a closer fit to Galatians 3:6-14 if we focus on examples where the 'something else' *claims* to be especially honouring to God, but in reality is not.

What must this include? Most preachers will jump quickly to an attack on 'legalism' of some sort: some attempt to gain favour from God from good works that is *separate* to, or replaces, a humble dependency on Christ. There may be some warrant in this, as we shall return to in a moment, but this is certainly not the only possibility: there are many others and some of them very close to home. I guess an extreme and obvious example of someone abandoning Christ for something claiming to be honouring to God would be someone converting to another religion. But just as dangerous is a pluralism that *marginalises* the uniqueness of Christ and lumps all religions together. And this is endemic in the Christian community! It is made all the more attractive by the implication that such 'tolerance' must surely be honouring to God. There is much more that could be said here: many areas where doctrinal slippage may lead to downplaying the uniqueness of Christ and the exclusivity of salvation in him. Denying his substitutionary work is one obvious example (3:13 again!), but no doubt there are others.

Think next of the various Christian sub-cultures we know. We know what it is like to be a part of them, and how easy it can be for their peculiar pattern of activities to 'take over'. We can be very busy, doing many things apparently honouring to God, but have no love for Jesus at all. For many of us, this will be very close to home indeed.

Thinking more widely though, now more at the fringes of the Christian community and beyond, I think we still need to be attacking religiosity and legalism. I was recently 'door-knocking' for one afternoon on a Christian mission in Western Sydney and very struck by the uniformity of responses (when there was a response). Time and time again if people wanted to say 'No thank you', they would say, 'Sorry, we're Catholics.' Or, if they *really* wanted us to go away, they would say, 'Sorry, we're *strict* Catholics.' And if people did get talking, and we asked how they might be acceptable to God, they would say 'By being good, I guess,' or, 'By keeping the ten commandments.' It was almost comical in its predictability! If these things were not *quite* the issue in Galatia, they certainly are now. This is the 'folk theology' of our day, as it has been in many other times: go to church or be good-*ish* — either will do. So the task remains in our day to disabuse such people of their status before God and tell them that

> ...Christ redeemed us from the curse of the law by becoming a curse for us — for it is written, 'Cursed is everyone who is hanged on a tree' — so that in Christ Jesus the blessing of Abraham might come to the Gentiles, so that we might receive the promised Spirit through faith.

Bibliography

Abrams, M.H. *A Glossary of Literary Terms (5th Ed.)*. New York: Holt, Rinehart, and Winston, 1988.

Barr, James. *The Semantics of Biblical Language*. Oxford: Oxford University Press, 1961.

Baxter, Richard. *The Reformed Pastor*. 1656. Edinburgh: Banner of Truth, 1974.

Betz, Hans Dieter. *Galatians: A Commentary on Paul's Letter to the Churches in Galatia*. Hermeneia. Philadelphia: Fortress Press, 1979.

Bird, Michael F. *The Saving Righteousness of God: Studies on Paul, Justification and the New Perspective*. Paternoster Biblical Monographs. Milton Keynes: Paternoster, 2007.

Dunn, James D. G. *A Commentary of the Epistle to the Galatians*. Black's New Testament Commentaries. London: A&C Black, 1993.

Dunn, James D. G. *Jesus, Paul and the Law: Studies in Mark and Galatians*. London: SPCK, 1990.

Edwards, Jonathan. *Freedom of the Will*. Ed. P Ramsey. The Works of Jonathan Edwards, Vol. 1. New Haven and London: Yale University Press, 1985; first published 1754.

Esser, Hans-Helmut. *Law*. Vol. 2 of *New International Dictionary of New Testament Theology*.

Frame, John M. *The Doctrine of the Knowledge of God*. Grand Rapids, Michigan: Baker Books, 1987.

Hansen, G. Walter. *Abraham in Galatians: Epistolary and Rhetorical Contexts*. Journal for the Study of the New Testament Supplement Series 29. Sheffield: JSOT Press, 1989.

Hays, Richard B. *The Faith of Jesus Christ: The Narrative Substructure of Galatians 3:1–4:11*. SBL Dissertation Series 56. Chico, California: Scholar's Press, 1983.

Jeffery, Steve, Mike Ovey, and Andrew Sach. *Pierced for Our Transgressions: Rediscovering the Glory of Penal Substitution*. Nottingham: IVP, 2007.

Jensen, Peter. "Teaching Doctrine as Part of the Pastor's Role." Pp. 47–74 in *Interpreting God's Plan: Biblical Theology and the Pastor*. Ed. R. J. Gibson. Adelaide: Openbook and Paternoster Press, 1998.

Kern, Philip H. Rhetoric and Galatians: Assessing an Approach to Paul's Epistle. Society for New Testament Studies Monograph Series 101. Cambridge: Cambridge University Press, 1998.

Longenecker, Richard N. *Galatians*. Word Biblical Commentary Vol. 41. Dallas, Texas: Word Books, 1990.

Manchester, Simon. "Preaching with Biblical Confidence." *The Briefing (UK Ed.)*, no. 350 (2007): 22–26.

Martyn, J. Louis. *Galatians: A New Translation and Commentary*. The Anchor Bible Vol. 33A. New York: Doubleday, 1997.

Matlock, R. Barry. "The Arrow and the Web: Critical Reflections on a Narrative Approach to Paul." Pp. 44–57 in *Narrative Dynamics in Paul: A Critical Assessment*. Ed. Bruce W. Longenecker. Louisville, London: Westminster John Knox Press, 2002.

Moo, Douglas J. "Israel and the Law in Romans 5–11: Interaction with the New Perspective." Pp. 185–216 in *Justification and Variegated Nomism: Volume 2 – the Paradoxes of Paul*. Eds D.A. Carson, Peter T. O'Brien, and Mark A. Seifrid. Grand Rapids, Michigan: Baker Academic, 2004.

Murray, John. *Redemption Accomplished and Applied*. Grand Rapids: Eerdmans, 1955.

Piper, John. *The Future of Justification: A Response to N. T. Wright*. Wheaton, Illinois: Crossway Books, 2007.

Powlison, David. *Seeing with New Eyes: Counseling and the Human Condition Through the Lens of Scripture*. Phillipsburg, N.J.: P&R Pub., 2003.

Poythress, Vern S. *Symphonic Theology: The Validity of Multiple Perspectives in Theology*. Grand Rapids, Michigan: Zondervan, 1987.

Sanders, E. P. *Paul and Palestinian Judaism: A Comparison of Patterns of Religion*. London: SCM Press, 1977.

Silva, Moisés. *Interpreting Galatians: Explorations in Exegetical Method*. Grand Rapids, Michigan: Baker Academic, 2001.

Spurgeon, Charles H. "The Curse Removed." *Metropolitan Tabernacle Pulpit* 57 (1911).

Tolmie, D. Francois. *Persuading the Galatians: A Text-Centred Rhetorical Analysis of a Pauline Letter*. Wissenschaftliche Untersuchungen Zum Neuen Testament. 2 Reihe. 190. Tübingen: Mohr Siebeck, 2005.

Turretin, Francis. *Institutes of Elenctic Theology*. Edited by James T. Dennison. Translated by George Musgrave Giger. Phillipsburg, N.J.: P&R Publishing, 1992-c1997.

Vanhoozer, Kevin J. *Is There a Meaning in This Text? The Bible, the Reader and the Morality of Literary Knowledge*. Leicester: IVP/Apollos, 1998.

Watson, Francis. "Is There a Story in These Texts?" Pp. 231–39 in *Narrative Dynamics in Paul: A Critical Assessment*. Ed. Bruce W. Longenecker. Louisville, London: Westminster John Knox Press, 2002.

Watson, Francis. *Paul and the Hermeneutics of Faith*. London, New York: T & T Clark International, 2004.

Watson, Francis. *Text, Church and World: Biblical Interpretation in Theological Perspective*. Grand Rapids, Michigan: Eerdmans, 1994.

Willits, Joel. "Context Matters: Paul's Use of Leviticus 18:5 in Galatians 3:12." *Tyndale Bulletin* 54, no. 2 (2003): 105–22.

Wright, N. T. *The Climax of the Covenant: Christ and the Law in Pauline*

Theology. Minneapolis: Fortress Press, 1993.

Wright, N. T. "The Cross and the Caricatures: A Response to Robert Jenson, Jeffrey John and a New Volume Entitled 'Pierced for Our Transgressions'." Fulcrum, 2007. Http://www.fulcrum-anglican.org.uk/news/2007/20070423wright.cfm?doc=205.

Wright, N. T. *What Saint Paul Really Said: Was Paul of Tarsus the Real Founder of Christianity?* Grand Rapids, Michigan: Eerdmanns, 1997.

Latimer Publications

Latimer Publications

LATIMER PUBLICATIONS